RUTH
A Love Story

Linda Osborne

ISBN:-10: 0615894178
ISBN-13: 9780615894171

CONTENTS

PREFACE

✦

Who doesn't enjoy a good love story? We all do, don't we? Well in the Book of Ruth we have several love stories in one. We have the love of a daughter-in-law devoted to her mother-in-law, and that's a beautiful story. But then we have an even better love story—we have the story of a young and childless widow who finds herself loved by a man and ultimately fulfilled with a child, and that's a beautiful story, too. But then we have an even better story, because out of this love story we have a picture of the greatest love of all—the love of a father for his children—but not just any father, for any children—the love of the *heavenly Father* for His children—you and me—a love so great that He provided us with a Kinsman-Redeemer in His Son, Jesus Christ. "For God so loved the world, that He gave His only begotten Son, that whoever believes in Him should not perish, but have eternal life" (John 3:16).

Romans 8:28 says, "And we know that God causes all things to work together for good to those who love God, to those who are called according to His purpose." What could be a better verse to use as our theme for this study? We will see, as we ponder this portion of Scripture, that there is Sovereignty at work here, as we see Ruth, a Moabitess, brought by way of her tragic circumstances to Bethlehem (and you know the significance of Bethlehem!), where she meets and marries Boaz, through whom she bears a son who is in the line of King David and ultimately the Messiah. You see God causes *all things*—even the untimely death of a husband and the move to a foreign land—to work together for good to those who love Him. And there we have *another* love story in our book—the love of Ruth for the God of Israel.

.

GETTING STARTED

It is always good to begin a study by looking at the book as a whole. You may, therefore, want to read this entire letter in one sitting before you start your study verse by verse.

Your lesson will be divided into five-day increments. Each day you will be given a portion of Scripture to read and then you will be asked questions based on that passage and others relating to it. The questions will range from the *facts* of the passage to *personal application* and, finally, to questions that will encourage you to *dig a little deeper*. The *Digging Deeper* sections are optional —sort of like extra credit! Do them if you are able, as they will add depth to your study. Each lesson will have a *Memory Verse*—a verse which is applicable to the lesson at hand—for you to commit to memory. Finally, you'll be able to pull it all together in a personal overview of the passage you have been studying all week.

Let's not waste any more time. Let's get into our story!

RUTH 1

❖

Day 1
Daily Facts

Read Ruth 1, concentrating on verses 1-2

Right off the top, in verse one, we're given the condensed facts—sort of the "who, what, where, and when" of our story.

1. Although we aren't given an exact date, what is the time period in which this story is set? v. 1

    a. The main characters in the beginning of our story are listed in verse 1; their names are given in verse 2. List them here.

    b. Where is the main part of our story set? (The home of this family.)

    c. Where is the secondary location of the story?

d. So far we have the "when," the "who," and the "where" of our story. From verse 1, write a sentence stating the "what," or, in other words, the occasion of the story.

Names are significant in the Bible. They actually represent the people or the places to which they belong. Let's take a look at the meanings of the names in our story so far:

✢ Elimelech means *my God is King*
✢ Naomi means *pleasant.* In his commentary *All the Women of the Bible,* Herbert Lockyer says that her name is "suggestive of all that is charming, agreeable and attractive"; and that "we can understand Naomi having a nature corresponding to her name."
✢ Mahlon means *invalid.*
✢ Chilion means *pining.*
✢ Bethlehem means *house of bread.*
✢ Judah means *praise.*
✢ Moab means *washbowl.* J. Vernon McGee quotes Psalm 108:9 KJV, in which it says, "Moab is my washpot." He goes on to say that a paraphrase of what God says about Moab could be "Moab is my garbage can."

2. We can't draw hard conclusions here, but we can speculate: Considering the names of the cities involved, do you think it was a wise move on Elimelech's part to take his family to Moab?

We recall that Abraham left the country to which God had called him and traveled to Egypt, which is a type of the world, and that he got into trouble there.

a. What did God tell Isaac, when he, like Abraham, was confronted with a famine in the land? Genesis 26:1-2

Making It Personal

3. Could that be a word to you in the "famine" you are now facing (whether personal, financial, or otherwise)? Think this through and share your heart—what do those words mean to you in your place of difficulty?

    a. Have you ever stepped out of God's will because you were heading toward a situation you couldn't face? Share the results of that decision.

    b. What should you do when facing a "famine"?

Digging Deeper

It's thought that our story probably occurred early in the period of Judges because of the fact that Boaz is the son of Rahab, the woman who hid the Israelites who "spied out" the Promised Land.

4. Go back and scan the book of Judges to get an idea of the setting of our story—particularly chapters 3-8, as it may have been during the judgment of Ehud or Deborah, or in the days of Gideon, when Israel was in a time of famine. (The book of Judges is not written in chronological order.) Share anything significant you learn about this time in the history of Israel. For a defining statement you may want to look at the last verse in the book of Judges—Judges 21:25.

✤ Do your best to summarize today's passage in a couple of sentences.

Memory Verse

"Your people shall be my people, and your God, my God." Ruth 1:16

Day 2
Daily Facts
Read Ruth 1:3-7

1.   What were the sad results of the journey "down to" Moab?

✤ *verse 3—*

✤ *verse 4—*

✤ *verse 5—*

a.   Although we realize that this is the point Ruth comes into the story and therefore it actually becomes a high point, still, why would it have been a sad thing for the sons of Elimelech and Naomi to have married women of Moab? Deuteronomy 7:1-3

b.   Why might God have made this law? Can you think of any New Testament teachings that are similar to this?

5

✤ Orpah means *deer* or *fawn.*
✤ Ruth means *beauty, personality,* or *friendship.*

2.   What did Naomi decide to do after suffering such great loss in Moab? v. 6 What had she heard?

Bethlehem was once again the "house of bread"! Naomi was going home!

a.   What did the prophet Micah say about the city of Bethlehem? Micah 5:2 Share your understanding of what this verse refers to.

3.   Who left Moab with Naomi? v. 7

a.   Why might they have been inclined to go with her? (Think about her name.)

Although Ruth had no idea of the great event that was to take place in Bethlehem, it was part of God's sovereign plan that she leave Moab and journey on to Bethlehem, because *God causes all things to work together for good ...*

Making It Personal

4.   Is it at all possible that those circumstances in your life right now that you would love to turn away from could be part of the sovereign design of God to get you where He wants you for future blessing? Think about that for a moment and comment.

Digging Deeper

5. Let's take the verse Romans 8:28 and break it down into smaller parts. Take a moment to consider each part and then write a few words concerning the importance of each one—with your own difficult situation in mind.

✣ *And we know...*

✣ *That God causes...*

✣ *All things ...*

✣ *To work together for good ...*

✣ *To those who love God ...*

✣ *To those who are called according to His purpose ...*

✣ Do your best to summarize today's passage in a couple of sentences.

✣ Review your memory verse.

Day 3
Daily Facts
Read Ruth 1:8-14

1. What did Naomi direct her daughters-in-law to do? v. 8

The word used here for return has the meaning of *turn back, turn away,* or *retreat*.

    a. What do you think of when you hear the word *retreat* in this connotation? Is it usually a good thing?

    b. If they were to "retreat" from this journey into Judah, not only would they be going back to "their mothers' houses," but what else would they be going back to? (See also verse 15.)

    c. Was it really a good thing for Naomi to encourage them to return?

2. Obviously, Naomi's reasons for wanting them to go back were unselfish and loving. Share what you think some of her reasons might have been. (Think about the state of affairs for Naomi personally. Our passage offers some insight as well.)

    a. Considering the true and most important priorities of life, why would it still have been better for the women to return to Judah with Naomi?

3. Look for the love in our passage today (verses 8-14)—the love of Naomi for her daughters-in-law, and their love for her. Share what you find—including the blessings she spoke over them.

4. Obviously Naomi was a sad woman. Who wouldn't be? She lost her husband and her two sons. But we see a note of bitterness in this passage. What is it? v. 13

    a. Was Naomi looking at this correctly? Share your own thoughts (no right or wrong here).

Making It Personal

Sometimes the hand of the Lord has gone forth against you—perhaps your sorrowful situation is the result of bad moves and decisions on your own part, and the Lord steps in and corrects. Sometimes you are under spiritual attack by the adversary. Sometimes your situation is the result of just simply living in this world.

5. In any case, what is always the right thing to do? (See Naomi's example in verse 7b.)

Departing from your *physical* location isn't the answer here—unless the Lord directs you to do so—remember, "Don't go down to Egypt"! The example Naomi sets for us here is that she went back to where the Lord was—and that was Judah.

    a. 1 Samuel 30:1-6 gives us an example of David being in an extremely tight and distressful situation. Make note of what Scripture tells us he did.

    b. When we are in a tight place, more often than not we *have* to stay right where we are—we can't usually pick up and move someplace else! What would it look like for you to encourage yourself in the Lord right where you are today?

c. Are you doing these things in your place of difficulty?

Digging Deeper

✣ Do your best to summarize today's passage in a couple of sentences.

✣ Review your memory verse.

Day 4
Daily Facts
Read Ruth 1:15-22

1. As a result of the discussion Naomi had with the women, what seems to have happened to Orpah? v.15

   a. Would Ruth follow her example? Look back at verse 14 and remember what Ruth did.

2. What strong words did Ruth use to stop the pleading of Naomi? v. 16a

   a. Ruth went on to list five ways in which she would fully follow Naomi. List them here. vv. 16-17

1.
2.
3.
4.
5.

What a beautiful declaration of love this was. We must note the kind of woman Naomi had been and the kind of woman Ruth was. A very interesting side note here is that the origination of the marriage vow, *"Till death do we part,"* comes from Ruth's words to Naomi in this passage.

    b.   For those who are married, consider your marriage for a moment. Besides the religious aspect of Ruth's proclamation (some of you may have husbands who don't yet know the One True and Living God), have you made this kind of commitment to your husband? Does this area need some work?

3.   What do the words, "Your God shall be my God," imply about Ruth's relationship to the God of Israel?

    a.   Where did Ruth learn about this God?

We see here, once again, the reason that Ruth loved Naomi so much.

4.   What was the reaction of the people in Bethlehem to the arrival of Naomi and Ruth? v. 19 What question did the women ask?

    a.   What do you think they might have been thinking?

    b.   Describe Naomi from her response in verses 20-21.

5. What final piece of information are we given in verse 22b?

Making It Personal

Ruth made a commitment to go forward with Naomi into all and whatever that commitment would mean. Orpah went back.

6. Ponder the words in Luke 9:57-62, which remind us that the commitment to Christ is a commitment to go forward, no matter what the circumstances may be. Ponder also the words of Mark 8:34-36, which give us Christ's perception of a disciple. Write your thoughts about the strict message these words portray.

   Luke 9:57-62—

   Mark 8:34-36—

   a. From the teaching in these verses, which way are you looking and moving: forward or backward? If someone were to examine your life, would they recognize you as a disciple?

Digging Deeper

- Do your best to summarize today's passage in a couple of sentences.

- Review your memory verse.

Day 5
Overview of Ruth 1

Today we will be looking at the passage we have studied this week as a whole. The goal is to find the main lessons the Lord has for us from this chapter. Don't worry about being clever or profound—just do your best!

Find the Facts ...

1. See if you can state the *content* of this week's passage in a couple of sentences. You can use your daily summary statements to help you come up with one main theme or summary of the chapter. (Who is speaking, what is taking place, what is the main subject?)

Look for the Heart ...

2. What do you think is the main *lesson* of this chapter? (What spiritual truths are taught here? Look for a command, a word of exhortation, a promise, etc.)

Hear Him Speak ...

3. Look for a *personal application* from the content of this chapter. It should come from the lesson you got from the chapter (question 2). How will you apply the lesson to yourself?

4. Was there a particular verse that ministered to you this week? What was it and how did it minister to you?

5. Write out your memory verse *from memory*!

RUTH 2

"Now Naomi had a kinsman ..." And so begins the second chapter of Ruth. And with these words, we get the first hint of the wonderful thing that will soon take place for both Ruth and Naomi.

There were two laws in place for Israel that dealt with the poor. Both of them will come into play beginning in this chapter. The first one is found in Leviticus 19:9-10, in which God made provision for the physical needs of the poor. The second is found in Deuteronomy 25:5-6, which was another provision of God for His people, in particular in regard to the continuation of their lineage, but also in relation to their land (see also Leviticus 25:23-25). This one was especially important to the poor and the widowed.

Day 1
Daily Facts
Read Ruth 2, concentrating on verses 1-2

In chapter 2, another main character of our story is introduced. Boaz's name means *strength*.

1.   Share everything you learn about Boaz in verse 1.

Scripture tells us that Boaz was a man of great wealth. This verse can also be translated that he was a mighty, valiant man—which goes along with the meaning of his name. All in all, Boaz was a great man!

2.   What was it that Ruth wanted to do? v. 2

    a.   How did she ask Naomi this question?

Take a moment and think about what this might look like. Ruth wasn't being asked to come and do a job. She would be going into someone else's field (someone she didn't know and who didn't know her), walking behind their reapers and gathering what was left behind.

    b.   Do you think Ruth wanted to do this? Do you think she was excited about doing this? Why did she do it?

    c.   Name a few of Ruth's characteristics that you glean from verse 2.

3.   In a word, what was Ruth hoping to find that day? (Still verse 2.)

    a.   And here we have another one of Ruth's fine characteristics. Do you see what it is?

The word used for favor in the NASB and NKJV is translated "grace" in the KJV. Ruth was looking for grace!

Making It Personal

Ruth was looking for grace ... that doesn't seem like that big of a deal—or does it?

4. When you are in trying circumstances—maybe your finances are in bad shape, maybe your relationships are in bad shape, maybe you're just generally in bad shape—are you more often hopeful or hopeless? Be honest!

Scripture gives us a clue about just how important hopefulness (or maybe we should call it *faith*) is.

a. Write out the words of Hebrews 11:6.

b. See if you can break this verse down into three parts or phrases:

1.

2.

3.

c. Write each of these phrases from a personal perspective of what God wants from *you.*

1.

2.

3.

d. Now, share why it is important that you—a child of the Living God—be hopeful, even in the most trying of circumstances.

e. Ask the Lord to give you an opportunity this very week to be hopeful in the face of a disturbing matter, and then share with your group the difference it made. You might even be able to share the end result of the matter, because God often moves quickly when we act in faith rather than fear!

Digging Deeper

5. Do a word study on the word *grace*. You can use a regular dictionary, or you can use your Bible's index or a concordance to lead you on a study of this word throughout the Bible. Share with your group what you discover. You may also want to do a study on the word *faith*!

✤ Do your best to summarize today's passage in a couple of sentences.

Memory Verse

"… The God of Israel, under whose wings you have come to seek refuge." Ruth 2:12b

Day 2
Daily Facts
Read Ruth 2:3-9

At Ruth's request, Naomi said, "Go."

1.   What "happened to happen" as Ruth went to the fields to glean? v. 3

    a.   Do you think this really just *happened*? What really happened?

The meaning of this verse is also translated, "her chance chanced upon." The KJV says, "her hap (or chance) was to light upon a part of the field belonging unto Boaz …" Another way of saying this might be that she was *lucky* enough to end up in the field of Boaz.

    b.   Do you think the word luck belongs in the child of God's vocabulary? Why? (This is the important part!)

    c.   Relate this "happenstance" to the theme verse for our study— Romans 8:28.

    d.   What is the attribute of God that Ruth's "good fortune" makes you think of?

2.   Where had Boaz just come from? v. 4

a. Name a couple of things that you learn about the character of this man Boaz from verse 4.

3. What question did Boaz ask his servant? v. 5

Boaz had noticed Ruth! Yes, she was there in his field. Yes, she was a stranger, and it might have been a very normal thing for him to see her and ask about her—but isn't it possible that when his eyes landed upon this woman whose name means *beauty* that it was more than just a nonchalant question, that he was not only inquisitive but very much interested in the beautiful young stranger in his field? J. Vernon McGee thinks so. In fact, he is convinced that it was love at first sight!

a. Who was she, according to the servant? v. 6

b. What else did he tell Boaz? v. 7

4. After hearing who she was and what she was doing there, Boaz approached Ruth. Make a list of the things he said to her. vv. 8-9

a. Remember Ruth's hope of the morning? How had she received what she had hoped for?

Making It Personal

As we continue to ponder this passage of Scripture, let's go back for just a moment to Boaz's word to Ruth, "Do not go to glean in another field" (verse 8).

5. From a spiritual perspective, think of these words as being spoken to you by your Kinsman-Redeemer. What do they mean to you?

   a. Are you gleaning in any other fields? What would it mean to you personally to only gather in the field of your Lord?

Digging Deeper

6. The word glean means to *gather up*. The process of gleaning is one of the provisions the Lord made for His people. Look up Leviticus 19:9-10 and share what you learn there. Who, according to verse 10, was this provision for?

   a. Deuteronomy 24:19 gives us a further understanding about this law. Who were mentioned in this case as recipients of this provision?

✦ Do your best to summarize today's passage in a couple of sentences.

✦ Review your memory verse.

Day 3
Daily Facts
Read Ruth 2:10-16

1. Describe Ruth's reaction to Boaz's words. v. 10

Can you imagine how overwhelmed Ruth must have been? She might have even been afraid when he approached her—he was the master of this field—perhaps she thought he would scold her for being there.

    a.   What specifically did Ruth call herself in verse 10?

Ruth's specific question to Boaz, in the midst of his obvious favor, was, "Why have I found favor in your sight that you should take notice of me, since I am a foreigner?" Ruth wasn't of any of the tribes of Israel. She was a Gentile. She was a Moabitess. She was a stranger and a foreigner to the promises of God, yet she was favored by her future kinsman-redeemer.

2. Look at Ephesians 2:11-13 and see if you can liken your own situation to the one in which Ruth found herself.

    a.   In whom have you been brought near? Considering our story, who is He?

3. How did Boaz respond to Ruth's posture and words in verse 10? v. 11

a. Verse 12 is wonderful. In the first part of the verse, Boaz speaks a word of blessing over Ruth. What is it?

b. In what beautiful manner does he describe her relationship with God?

Maybe Boaz had heard that Ruth had given her heart to Israel's God. Or maybe he could just sense it. But rightly did he speak!

4. What invitation did Boaz give to Ruth at mealtime? v. 14

a. Look carefully at this verse. Who does it appear served (or fed) Ruth?

5. What did Boaz command his servants concerning Ruth? v. 15

a. What other provision did he make for her? v. 16

Making It Personal

6. Boaz recognized that Ruth was seeking refuge under the wings of the Most High. Are you like Ruth? Have you placed yourself under His wings and do you seek *refuge* there?

a. Using a regular dictionary, define the word *refuge*.

In Hebrew "seeking refuge" is *chacah*, and it has several meanings: to confide in, to have hope, make refuge, and to (put) trust. But primarily it means the most wonderful thing—it means to *flee for protection*.

b. Are you trying to handle your own problems? Do you ever find yourself afraid to go to the Lord, thinking maybe you've already asked Him for help too many times or that your fears and your problems are too petty to bother Him with? Is it time for you to *flee for protection*—looking to your heavenly Father for the need in your life right now?

c. Look at Psalm 37:39-40 and notice from verse 40 *why* it is that the Lord helps and delivers those who are in need.

Digging Deeper

7. Ruth had placed herself under the wings of the God *of Israel*. If you are a Christian, you have done the same. See if you can relate to Ruth's words, "since I am a foreigner," in this regard. See Romans 11:17-24 for help.

✝ Do your best to summarize today's passage in a couple of sentences.

✝ Review your memory verse.

Day 4
Daily Facts
Read Ruth 2:17-23

1. What was the result of Ruth's hard work that day? (See if you can discover what this measurement is equivalent to.)

   a. What did she take home to her mother-in-law? v. 18

2. Naomi realized right away that Ruth had found favor—what word did she speak toward the one who had favored her? v. 19

   a. What was Naomi's reaction to the name of Boaz? v. 20a

   b. In Naomi's words blessing Boaz, we see a hint of a change in her spirit. Compare her words in verse 20a to her words in 1:20-21. What small change seems to be taking place?

3. Who was Boaz, according to Naomi? v. 20b

The Hebrew word for closest relative or nearest kin is *gaal*, and it means literally "one who has the right to redeem."

a. Look at Deuteronomy 25:5-6 for the law God provided the one who was widowed without a child to carry on the name of her deceased husband.

This law stated a *duty* of the nearest kin. "He *shall* go in to her and take her to himself as wife ..."

b. The immediate reason for this law was to provide an heir, so that her husband's name would not be blotted out. Can you think of some other things this provision made for the widow herself?

4. How did Naomi counsel Ruth in regard to this situation? v. 22

a. How long did Ruth remain in the fields of Boaz?

Making It Personal

Ruth needed to be redeemed—and here was the promise of a redeemer. Help for Ruth was on its way! Did the rulers of Moab have such a law in place for a poor widowed woman? The God of Israel did. The world teaches us that "God helps those who help themselves." God's Word teaches us that "God helps those who can't help themselves."

5. Do you need help today? The word *gaal* means redeem, buy back, purchase, ransom, revenge. Your Redeemer not only made provision for you once and for all, He wants to redeem you each and every time you need Him. Won't you go to Him today and seek grace? Ruth looked for grace, and because she looked she found it!

Digging Deeper

✤ Do your best to summarize today's passage in a couple of sentences.

✤ Review your memory verse.

Day 5
Overview of Ruth 2

Today we will be looking at the passage we have studied this week as a whole. The goal is to find the main lessons the Lord has for us from this chapter. Don't worry about being clever or profound—just do your best!

Find the Facts ...

1. See if you can state the *content* of this week's passage in a couple of sentences. You can use your daily summary statements to help you come up with one main theme or summary of the chapter. (Who is speaking, what is taking place, what is the main subject?)

Look for the Heart ...

2. What do you think is the main *lesson* of this chapter? (What spiritual truths are taught here? Look for a command, a word of exhortation, a promise, etc.)

Hear Him Speak ...

3. Look for a *personal application* from the content of this chapter. It should come from the lesson you got from the chapter (question 2). How will you apply the lesson to yourself?

4. Was there a particular verse that ministered to you this week? What was it and how did it minister to you?

5. Write out your memory verse *from memory*!

RUTH 3

✤

In today's chapter, things begin to move forward, as Naomi, the wise mother-in-law, gives Ruth a little nudge in the right direction. Remember, Ruth is a Moabitess. She wouldn't have known the customs of Israel. Did she think they were a little strange? Probably, and we certainly may—but again, we realize that they were the norm in those days. Just think what they would have thought of some of our customs today!

Day 1
Daily Facts
Read Ruth 3:1-5

1. What did Naomi desire for her daughter-in-law? v. 1

    a. That word translated "security" is the same word translated "rest" in Ruth 1:9. According to that verse, what did Naomi want for Ruth?

b. The word for "well" in verse 1 is *yatah*, and it means (among other things) "to make well, beautiful, sound, happy, successful, right, to be accepted, to amend, to benefit, and to please." From these thoughts in verse 1, what was it that Naomi wanted for Ruth?

c. Things were going pretty well for Naomi. We see in Ruth 2:23 that Ruth worked gleaning in the fields all day—presumably bringing home food for her and Naomi each night and that she lived with her mother-in-law—so Naomi wasn't alone. What positive trait do we see in Naomi in the beginning of our chapter today?

Ruth had been working in Boaz's field for around six to eight weeks by now, and harvest season was drawing to a close. The opportunity for Ruth to see Boaz every day was coming to an end. Naomi knew the time had come for Ruth to move.

2. What information did Naomi give to Ruth at this particular time? v. 2

a. What instructions did she give her about:

How to look—verse 3

How to act—verse 4

b. What kinds of feelings do you think Ruth might have had about this suggestion (what kinds of feelings would you have had)?

3. How did Ruth answer Naomi? What do you see about Ruth's relationship to Naomi from this verse? v. 5

    a. How is Ruth an example to you here?

Making It Personal

4. Considering Naomi's situation, it probably wouldn't have been easy for her to let Ruth go. How do you think you would have done if you were in her shoes? (Think of it from the perspective of allowing your husband or child to get involved in something that would take them away from you much of the time or of encouraging a friend to do something that would change the nature of your relationship.)

    a. Naomi treated Ruth how Ruth had treated her. See if you can share how that was.

There aren't too many sins that are harder to die to than the sins of "self." Selfishness, self-centeredness, self-will, self-reliance, self-righteousness, self-consciousness, self-conceit, self-love, self-pity.

5. Do you struggle with anything on that list? Be honest with yourself and share it here—or you may come up with another "self" sin that isn't even on our list!

6. Is there anyone with whom you are being selfish right now? Let Naomi be an example to you. Determine that you will repent (turn and go in the other direction) and handle your situation selflessly rather than selfishly. Share any thoughts you have about this.

Digging Deeper

✸ Do your best to summarize today's passage in a couple of sentences.

Memory Verse

"Spread the corner of your garment over me, since you are a kinsman-redeemer." Ruth 3:9 (NIV)

Day 2
Daily Facts
Read Ruth 3:6-13

1. How obedient was Ruth? v. 6

    a. Share exactly what took place. vv. 7-8

    b. See if you can come up with some words to describe the move that Ruth made here.

2. In response to the question, "Who are you?" Ruth revealed herself to Boaz. What beautiful statement did she make, showing Boaz exactly why she was there? v. 9b

Ruth was, in effect, making a marriage proposal!

   a. Think of the covenant of marriage. How is it that a man "spreads the corner of his garment over his bride"?

   b. If you are married, are you letting your husband spread the corner of his garment over you?

3. What did Boaz see the "proposal" of Ruth to be, and what did he say? v. 10

We have to think that Boaz most likely had the hope of marrying Ruth on his mind already. Probably from the first day he saw her! Of course we can only speculate, but do you think it might be possible that Boaz was afraid to approach her or make his desire known because he wasn't a young man? Might he have been afraid of rejection? Whatever the case, there was no reluctance on his part now!

   a. What was Boaz's answer to Ruth's proposal? v. 11

   b. What was the only possible problem in this situation? vv. 12-13

Making it personal

Sometimes a step forward can take a great deal of faith. I think we can safely say that Ruth took a great step of faith in this situation. She couldn't have known what Boaz would say, she was exposing herself in the most vulnerable way. But it would only be through such a great step of faith that such a great opportunity would be gained.

Sometimes, like Ruth, we hold the key to our happiness in our own hands and the gate will not begin to open until we approach it and unlock it with the key of faith.

4. Is there any prospect in your life right now in which you are held back by fear?

    a. What would the "key of faith" look like in your situation?

Streams in the Desert says, "There are times when it takes strength simply to sit still, but there are also times when we are to move forward with a confident step."[1] And in another devotion it says, "Faith that goes forward triumphs."[2]

    b. Fear keeps us bound up and useless. Are you ready to "go forward"? Share what God is speaking to you.

Digging Deeper

5. We've thought of the words of Ruth in the context of the marriage relationship. Now, spend some time thinking of them with regard to our Kinsman-Redeemer, Jesus Christ. What does it look like for Him to spread the corner of His garment over you, His bride? See if you can come up with some Scriptural basis for your thoughts.

✤ Do your best to summarize today's passage in a couple of sentences.

✤ Review your memory verse.

Day 3

Daily Facts

Read Ruth 3:11

Making It Personal

Today we will be looking at only one verse—verse 11, and only one word in that verse—the word *virtuous* (NKJV). This entire day of our lesson will be a personal day. Enjoy![3]

1. Let's look at some of the traits of the virtuous woman in Proverbs 31 and compare them to our virtuous Ruth. Share briefly what you glean from each verse noted:

✤ Devoted to her family

Ruth 1:15-18

Proverbs 31:10-12, 23

Are you "devoted" to your family? How does that look for you?

✤ Delighting in her work

Ruth 2:2

Proverbs 31:13

Share a way that you "delight" in your work.

✤ Diligent in her labor

Ruth 2: 7, 17, 23

Proverbs 31:14-18, 19-21, 24, 27

Are "diligent" in your labor? Share an example.

✢ Dedicated to godly speech

Ruth 2:10, 13

Proverbs 31:26

In what way have you "dedicated" yourself to godly speech?

✢ Dependent on God

Ruth 2:12

Proverbs 31:25b, 30

Share a recent example of your "dependence" on God.

✢ Dressed with care

Ruth 3:3

Proverbs 31:22, 25a

Is modesty and tidiness important to you? Share a change in this area you have made.

✣ Discreet with men

Ruth 3:6-13

Proverbs 31:11, 12, 23

Can you think of an example of how you are "discreet" with men?

✣ Delivering blessings

Ruth 4:14, 15

Proverbs 31:28, 29, 31

Share a recent example of "delivering" a blessing. (It's okay—go ahead and share it!)

2. Do you consider yourself a virtuous woman? In which of these traits do you consider yourself strong?

3. Choose one of these traits that you need to work on, and share how you think you might do that.

Day 4
Daily Facts
Read Ruth 3:14-18

1. What careful measure did Boaz take so that Ruth would suffer no embarrassment—particularly since there was another party involved? v. 14

   a. What token did Boaz give to Ruth? v. 15

This was actually a very large gift. It amounted to possibly 15 gallons of barley. It was probably as much as he could give her that she would be able to get home!

2. We can only imagine Naomi's eagerness to hear the details of the evening. How do you think Ruth might have shared what took place? v. 16

   a. Who did Ruth say the gift of barley was actually for? v. 17

3. Naomi had been married and she had two sons. What did she know about men in this situation? v. 18

Making It Personal

Wait. Boy can that be a hard word to hear! We talked on an earlier day about moving forward, but here we see that sometimes we have to wait—and that can really be hard! But just as important as it is to move forward when God says move, it is equally important that we wait when He says wait.

4. Have you ever moved forward in something that you *knew* the Lord was prompting you to do but then you found you had to wait? What do you experience when you have to wait on the Lord?

    a. Have you had an experience of waiting on the Lord and afterwards being thankful that you waited? Share the encouragement with your group.

    b. Are you waiting on the Lord for something right now? What kind of a heart attitude should you cultivate during this time?

Digging Deeper

5. If you are in a place of waiting right now, then these verses may be of benefit to you. Look each one up and note its significance. Perhaps there will be one or two that will help you through your period of waiting.

Psalm 27:14

Psalm 37:7a, 9

Psalm 130:5-8

Isaiah 40:31

Isaiah 49:23b

Habakkuk 2:3

✣ Do your best to summarize today's passage in a couple of sentences.

✣ Review your memory verse.

Day 5

Overview of Ruth 3

Today we will be looking at the passage we have studied this week as a whole. The goal is to find the main lessons the Lord has for us from this chapter. Don't worry about being clever or profound—just do your best!

Find the Facts ...

1. See if you can state the *content* of this week's passage in a couple of sentences. You can use your daily summary statements to help you come up with one main theme or summary of the chapter. (Who is speaking, what is taking place, what is the main subject?)

Look for the Heart ...

2. What do you think is the main *lesson* of this chapter? (What spiritual truths are taught here? Look for a command, a word of exhortation, a promise, etc.)

Hear Him Speak…

3. Look for a *personal application* from the content of this chapter. It should come from the lesson you got from the chapter (question 2). How will you apply the lesson to yourself?

4. Was there a particular verse that ministered to you this week? What was it and how did it minister to you?

5. Write out your memory verse *from memory!*

RUTH 4

Just as Ruth moved forward at her mother-in-law's prompting, Boaz immediately moves forward to fulfill his promise to Ruth. There is excitement in the air! Can you imagine how Boaz must have been feeling? But mingled in with that excitement there was probably a significant amount of anxiety, as Boaz considered the fact that someone else may want Ruth. But this story has a happy ending, as we will soon see!

Day 1

Digging Deeper

Scan Ruth 1—4

Just as last week we considered the virtues of Ruth, today we will be looking at the virtues of Boaz, the man who "went up to the gate and sat down there ..." ready to fulfill his promise. Today we will begin by *Digging Deeper*—which is always a little more challenging![1]

1. See if you can write a few words relating Boaz to each of the virtues listed below. Share references from Ruth 1–4 if you are able:

✤ Diligent—

✤ Friendly—

✤ Merciful—

✤ Godly—

✤ Encouraging—

✤ Generous—

✤ Kind—

✤ Discreet—

✤ Faithful—

2. If you are a single woman hoping one day to be married, how important is this list of traits to you? Which one, for you, is most important?

    a. If you are a married woman, do you see any qualities on this list that describe your husband? Have you praised him lately for the characteristics of virtue that you see in his life? If not, could you start today?

    b. Are there any qualities on this list in which your husband is lacking? (Don't write them down or share them in your group—just take mental note of them.) How might you help him to grow in these areas? See if you can come up with some practical ways—but also see 1 Peter 3:1 (the Amplified version is especially good)!

Memory Verse

"And we know that God causes all things to work together for good to those who love God, to those who are called according to His purpose." Romans 8:28

Day 2

Daily Facts

Read Ruth 4:1-8

1. As soon as it was morning, Boaz headed for the city gate—share if you can the significance of the city gate (if you don't already know, see if you can discern it from the events recorded in these verses).

    a. What important thing happened there for Boaz? v. 1

    b. Do you think this was just happenstance or coincidence? What do you think was happening here?

    c. As Boaz asked the relative to sit down, what else did he do? v. 2

The number ten is important here. Normally two or three witnesses were sufficient to attest to a bargain being made. But in important matters, it was proper to have ten. Boaz wasn't taking any chances!

2. Notice the proposal Boaz made at first. What did it concern, and what important fact did he leave out? vv. 3-4

a. What was the relative's response?

b. Imagine what Boaz must have been thinking right then! But he had a "card up his sleeve" so to speak. What was that? v. 5

c. Now, what was the relative's response?

3. How was the transaction confirmed? vv. 7-8

Praise the Lord! Life was good! God was good! Boaz was blessed!

Making It Personal

In his wonderful book *Great Women of the Bible*, Clarence E. Macartney says that the story of Ruth "yields two great and timeless truths." One, he says, is providence, and he makes the point that, "Great events turn upon the hinges of little happenings." He goes on to say, "When you look back you see how life has been made up of happenings like that. Had you gone east instead of west, taken a morning train instead of an evening train, gone around another corner, met another person, life could not have been what it has been."

4. See if you can think of something that happened in your past (a corner turned) that changed your destiny.

a. Can you think of anything about your past life-experiences that have made you the person you are today?

The other great and timeless truth Macartney sees in Ruth is the power of choice and decision. This close relative of Elimelech made a bad choice (notice that this one who might have been in the genealogy of Jesus Christ is not even named). Orpah made a bad choice, but Ruth made an eternally good choice, choosing the God of Israel. And Boaz made an eternally good choice, choosing to redeem Ruth!

5. See if you can think of at least two choices you have made in life that have made an eternal difference.

Digging Deeper

6. Look carefully at our passage today and see if you can recognize some of the sacrifices that Boaz made in order to "redeem" Ruth. Use the following verses for your answer, as well as anything else you might come up with.

Deuteronomy 23:3 with Ruth 4:5:

Ruth 4:6:

Ruth 4:10:

Your thoughts:

✦ Do your best to summarize today's passage in a couple of sentences.

✦ Review your memory verse.

Day 3
Daily Facts
Read Ruth 4:9-17

Here we have Boaz at the gate with the closer relative, the ten elders, and "all the people." Presumably by this time there had gathered a small crowd of onlookers, perhaps trying to listen in on the important matter that was taking place at the city gate that day.

1. After the negotiations were complete, share the announcement Boaz made to all who were around.

verse 9

verse 10

Boaz thoroughly fulfilled his role as kinsman-redeemer.

   a. What three words of confirmation did the people say in response? v. 11a

2. What "blessing" did the witnesses speak over this union? v. 11

Rachel and Leah were the mothers of the twelve tribes of Israel—in verse 11 we see that they are remembered as "building" the house of Israel.

    a.   This was probably a common blessing to speak over the marriage of a Jewish man and woman but probably not so common to speak over a Jewish man marrying a Moabite woman. We saw the problem in Deuteronomy 23:3. What do you think made the difference in this case?

    b.   What an interesting choice of words that these witnesses used: "May you achieve wealth in Ephrathah and become famous in Bethlehem." Although they could never have known it at the time, what were they doing as they spoke these words?

3.   What second word of blessing did the witnesses speak over this union? v. 12

Perez was the ancestor of the people of Bethlehem—in the line of Judah, in the line of Christ.

4.   What was the happy ending to our story, as recorded in verse 13?

5.   What did the women say to Naomi at the birth of her grandson? v. 14

Again we see a word of prophecy! They wouldn't have known what they were doing, except that perhaps this was a common blessing spoken at the birth of a child. We remember that they would have been looking for the Messiah to be born, and perhaps as they spoke these very words there was a hint of that thought.

    a.   What else did they hope this child would be to Naomi? v. 15

    b.   How was this proven to be the case in verses 16-17?

Another interesting note: "They" named him Obed. Who were they? It seems to have been the neighbor women—Naomi's friends—who named him! The name Obed means "servant" or "worshiper."

Making it Personal

6.   Let's go back and pick up the threads of Naomi's story as it is told to us in this book:

Ruth 1:20

✦ Remember that Naomi's name means pleasant. After Naomi's loss in Moab, what did she call herself?

✦ How did she see the Lord's dealings with her?

Ruth 1:21

✦ How had Naomi "gone out"?

✦ How had she come back?

✤ Again, how did she see the Lord's dealings with her?

✤ Is Naomi "empty" any longer? (See how each verse reveals this.)

Ruth 4:14

Ruth 4:15a

Ruth 4:15b

Ruth 4:16

Ruth 4:17

✤ What do you think Naomi's testimony became in regard to Romans 8:28?

✤ Do you have a testimony like this?

Digging Deeper

We are going to spend time on the genealogy of Jesus in our next day of study, but for now, let's do just a little background work. Let's look back at the circumstances of the birth of Perez, Judah's son, both of whom are in the line of the Messiah.

7. Read Genesis 38 and make a few notes on what you learn about Judah and the birth of Perez.

a. What do you learn in this chapter about the line through which God brought His Son into this world?

✤ Do your best to summarize today's passage in a couple of sentences.

✤ Review your memory verse.

Day 4
Digging Deeper
Read Ruth 4:18-22

What a fitting way to end our study of Ruth—with a genealogy pointing to the One who is truly the main character of our story and every other story in the Bible as well! We're going to be looking at this entire day from the vantage point of *Digging Deeper*—so it might prove to be a little more challenging—but hopefully well worth it!

1. Write out the genealogy in list form as it is given in verses 18-22.

2. Now spend some time studying the genealogy given in Matthew 1. Put a bookmark there, as we will be referencing it throughout our study today.

We quickly pick up the thread of Ruth 4:18-22 after first reading of Abraham (the father of the faith!), Isaac (the promised son!), Jacob (the father of the 12 patriarchs!), and Judah (the patriarch through whose line Jesus would be born!).

    a.   What further piece of information do you note here about the birth of our character Boaz? Matthew 1:5

    b.   Go back to Joshua 2:1-21 and 6:22-25 and share a little bit of what you find there about Boaz's mother.

3.   Our genealogy in Ruth takes us to David, but leaves us there. Who was David according to our Matthew genealogy? Matthew 1:6

    a.   David was such a key figure in the line of Christ. What does I Chronicles 17:11-14 tell us was promised to him? What exactly did this mean?

The line to Christ went through David's son Solomon. David had other sons—but this is the line through which God chose to bring Christ into this world.

    b.   See the prophecy of this in 1 Chronicles 22:9-10.

c. What do you learn about Solomon's history in Matthew's genealogy? 1:6

d. Look back at 2 Samuel 11 and 12:15-25 and see the occasion of Solomon's birth.

4. Besides the young Mary, we see three women mentioned in Matthew's genealogy. Share the significant thing you have learned about each one of them.

Rahab—

Ruth—

The wife of Uriah—

a. Does it appear that God was concerned with maturity or spotlessness as He chose the people through whom He would bring His Son into this world?

b. Our study of Ruth has been "A Love Story." Share what you understand about the greatest lover—our God of love—through your study of Ruth.

Day 5
Overview of Ruth 4

Today we will be looking at the passage we have studied this week as a whole. The goal is to find the main lessons the Lord has for us from this chapter. Don't worry about being clever or profound—just do your best!

Find the Facts ...

1. See if you can state the *content* of this week's passage in a couple of sentences. You can use your daily summary statements to help you come up with one main theme or summary of the chapter. (Who is speaking, what is taking place, what is the main subject?)

Look for the Heart ...

2. What do you think is the main *lesson* of this chapter? (What spiritual truths are taught here? Look for a command, a word of exhortation, a promise, etc.)

Hear Him Speak ...

3. Look for a *personal application* from the content of this chapter. It should come from the lesson you got from the chapter (question 2). How will you apply the lesson to yourself?

4. Was there a particular verse that ministered to you this week? What was it and how did it minister to you?

5. Write out your memory verse *from memory*!

BIBLIOGRAPHY

Chapter 3
[1]See *Streams in the Desert*. By L.B. Cowman, p. 49
[2]IBID, p. 71
[3]Day 3 taken in part from *Women Who Love God,* by Elizabeth George, as she quotes John MacArthur from *Ruth: The Proverbs 31 Woman.*

Chapter 4
[1]Taken in part from *Women Who Love God,* by Elizabeth George.

ABOUT THE AUTHOR

Linda has dedicated her life to serving the Lord as a teacher, writer, and speaker. While teaching the Word of God, training leaders, and speaking at retreats and other women's ministry functions, she has also written curriculum for over 20 books of the Bible.

If you would be interested in having more information about her ministry, please visit her blog at www.lindaoborne.wordpress.com, or email her at myutmost1@aol.com.

Made in the USA
Lexington, KY
14 February 2015